Printed by Lightning Source, LLC., in the United States of America.

First printing, 2025.

Lightning Source, LLC.

1246 Heil Quaker Blvd,

La Vergne, TN, 37086

Instagram: jrodas001

Photo Credit: Jordan Rodas

i love you,
yesterday,
today,
and forever.

<u>Mental Health/Trigger Warning Disclaimer</u>

The contents of this book may be emotionally challenging for some and may invoke strong reactions. Many of the poems in this book are considered "dark" and depict potentially triggering subjects such as anxiety, death, depression, suicide, mental illness, and sexual assault.

If you are triggered at any point while you read, please stop and consult a mental health professional, or you can call or text the following hotline.

Suicide and Crisis Lifeline:

988

Preface

Everything you read plays on repeat in my head like a broken record every second of every day, yet I still manage to smile. Despite my outward appearance, I constantly fight against the hell in my mind. I do this with one singular intention: to stay alive. There are many more like me in this world, and if you relate to anything I write, you're one of them.

Waking up each morning tired of whatever existence you're living or surviving. You've found ways to hide these demons from those who care about you because you either don't want to worry them or you can't constantly try to explain the fact that the darkness never leaves you. Some think,

"I'm too tired to pretend."

Which is perfectly okay. I've gotten to that point too many times to count, and it's a usual way to guard your mental health. I know that it appears as though no one could help you with this mental illness, and to be frank, no one can. But, having at least one person you can vent to can be the difference between absolute loneliness and needed comfort. Don't be afraid to let someone in now and again. If you know anyone who struggles in these ways, communicate with them. Some need space, while others need constant reassurance.

In any case, I'm proof that you're not alone in your internal battles. We are born to die, yes, but we can choose whether or not to live life somewhere in between. Let these words echo and build a foundation you can always fall back on in your soul. Let the moments you've endured construct the blueprints of the tremendous human you are. Cherish those moments because they become memories, and then they become your myth.

A **moment** is defined as "a very brief period of time." Time slips away so quickly that the second we take a **moment** to breathe, we notice that months, years, or even decades have gone by.

Speaking from personal experience, twenty-six years elapsed in the blink of an eye. Elementary, middle, and high school were **momentary** blips on my life's timeline. My eight years of Active Duty service in the Air Force breezed by instantly. I've been married and divorced twice, both just transitory memories now.

Peering through the mirror of time, I remember that those memories were once **moments** that were laced with a litany of emotions. It is invaluable, I think, to try to keep your eyes as open as possible so you can experience and feel such emotions to their fullest extent. Some would agree with emotions like happiness, joy, lust, and faith, whereas others would be hesitant about emotions like loneliness, sadness, depression, and helplessness. Both are understandable in their own right, but "living" through these emotions later built the foundation of who we grow to be.

The person you are right now is *transcendent*, thanks to every **moment** you experience.

I love you yesterday, today, and forever.

the poetry,

exposed from my soul

i love you, yesterday, today, and forever

i'll be honest.
it took me some time,
but i'm finally happy.
without you.

i love you, yesterday, today, and forever

i held your hand for the first time.

it was slightly cold,

and a little sweaty

but in that instance

i knew,

my hand belonged in yours.

each breath was,

> slower

> > and slower.

until your lungs,

could no longer support

the weight of your existence.

> > > > one final exhale,

> > > separated soul from body.

your heart stopped beating

your blood ran cold

> > eternal slumber,

> where you were finally free.

i still reminisce about

how Vibrant your spirit was,

how Intense your passions were,

how Nuanced your outlook was,

how Captivating your determination was,

how Earnest your communication was,

how Neoteric your mind worked,

how Zealous you were towards your morals,

how Optimistic you were for our future.

they taught me i deserved better.

they taught me that the right person would stay and fight.

they taught me that consistency outweighs actions.

they taught me that the little things become lasting memories.

they taught me self-worth.

they taught me what true love wasn't.

they taught me i deserved better.

i still sleep on "my" side of the bed.

i still roll over,

reaching out my arm to hold you.

i still sit in the same spot on the couch,

right next to yours.

i still leave my arm on the center console,

where our hands would meet.

i still ordered your coffee,

so it seems like you're still here.

i haven't found hope in the vacancy,

but one day,

i will.

i would choose to ride through a hurricane of pain,
than to survive the storm of you leaving.

have you noticed yet?

now,
we're just a couple of strangers
who share some memories.

and it's all because of you.

"love" has never been just a feeling to me.

it was always a choice.

i chose to love you,

every day,

every night,

during the highs and lows,

despite your imperfections,

despite your appearance.

my love was my choice, my commitment, and my resolve.

you are the drug, and i am the addict,
forever trying to break the habit.
with every passing season, i always find a reason.
to love whichever version you've become.

i'm in love with a man

who loves someone else.

he calls him the nicknames he called me.

he holds his hand instead of mine.

he cares for him as he did for me.

he embraces him with all he has.

i'm in love with a man,

who loves someone else...

what a pathetic fucking story.

i watched the sun fall below the horizon.

his light streamed into a million rays

across the water's calm surface.

slowly sinking further and further,

dragging my heart into the ocean's depths.

day fades, and night paints the darkness

throughout everything in sight.

i won't see it,

the next sunrise.

i had plans.

i planned to clear my debt.

-     to clear your debt.
-     to get you a car.
-     to retire.
-     to travel the world with you.
-     to experience life with you.
-     to, one day, have kids with you.
-     our future together.

i planned to love you until the end of time.

i had plans, but you?

you only cared about yourself.

my poems appear sad on their surface,

but if you asked me on a deeper level,

i'd say they are full of life.

even as my innermost feelings paint these pages,

i fight tooth and nail every day

to stay alive.

which may seem trivial to the mentally healthy.

but for everyone who struggles like i do,

you know how easy it is to give in to the voices.

how easy it is to give up.

it only takes one moment of, "i'm tired of this shit,"

to stop existing.

i love you, yesterday, today, and forever

my final breath,

will mark the genesis,

of my happiness and freedom.

the demons were rapping in my ears today,

dropping bar after bar.

i think it's about time,

i listened to them and played to the beat of their drum.

my favorite song?

the symphony of words that leave your lips.

my favorite art?

the soft gleam of your eyes.

my favorite place?

beside you as to feel your warmth.

desire did not exist,

until i met you.

there have been many who commended me on

my stoicism throughout my suffering.

which only seems

to drive the knife deeper and deeper

as to cut the very fabric of my soul.

if,

comparison is the thief of joy.

then,

hope is the thief of happiness.

therefore,

i will never be joyful or happy.

because,

i hoped that, one day, you'd return to me.

my last time,

was with you.

to me, it was making love.

to you, it was just sex.

bittersweet emotions.

melancholy and nostalgia.

you were the last person

to see me that vulnerable.

night drew near,

the clock struck 11.

it was time.

pills washed down with whiskey.

making their home in my blood.

as my skin gets colder,

my breath stops –

my soul rekindles its flame.

when the sun comes up again,

look to the sky, and that's where i'll be.

i love you, yesterday, today, and forever

our game of chess

<u>beth's opening</u>

pawn to d4,

"do you want an open relationship?"

pawn to c4,

"there's a difference between sex and making love."

<u>the game continues…</u>

knight to e6,

"We could make extra money if we made content on Twitter."

pawn to g4,

"We could collab with cute guys."

<u>the endgame</u>

rook to f2,

"You're the one who wanted an open relationship."

king to d2,

"Opening our relationship proved to me that I would never be enough."

<u>borgov resigns. game over.</u>

when the time comes,

i'll greet *Death* as an old friend.

we'll sit and trade stories.

laugh at memories.

cringing at the embarassing times.

then *Death* and i will part ways

as i take apo solon's hand.

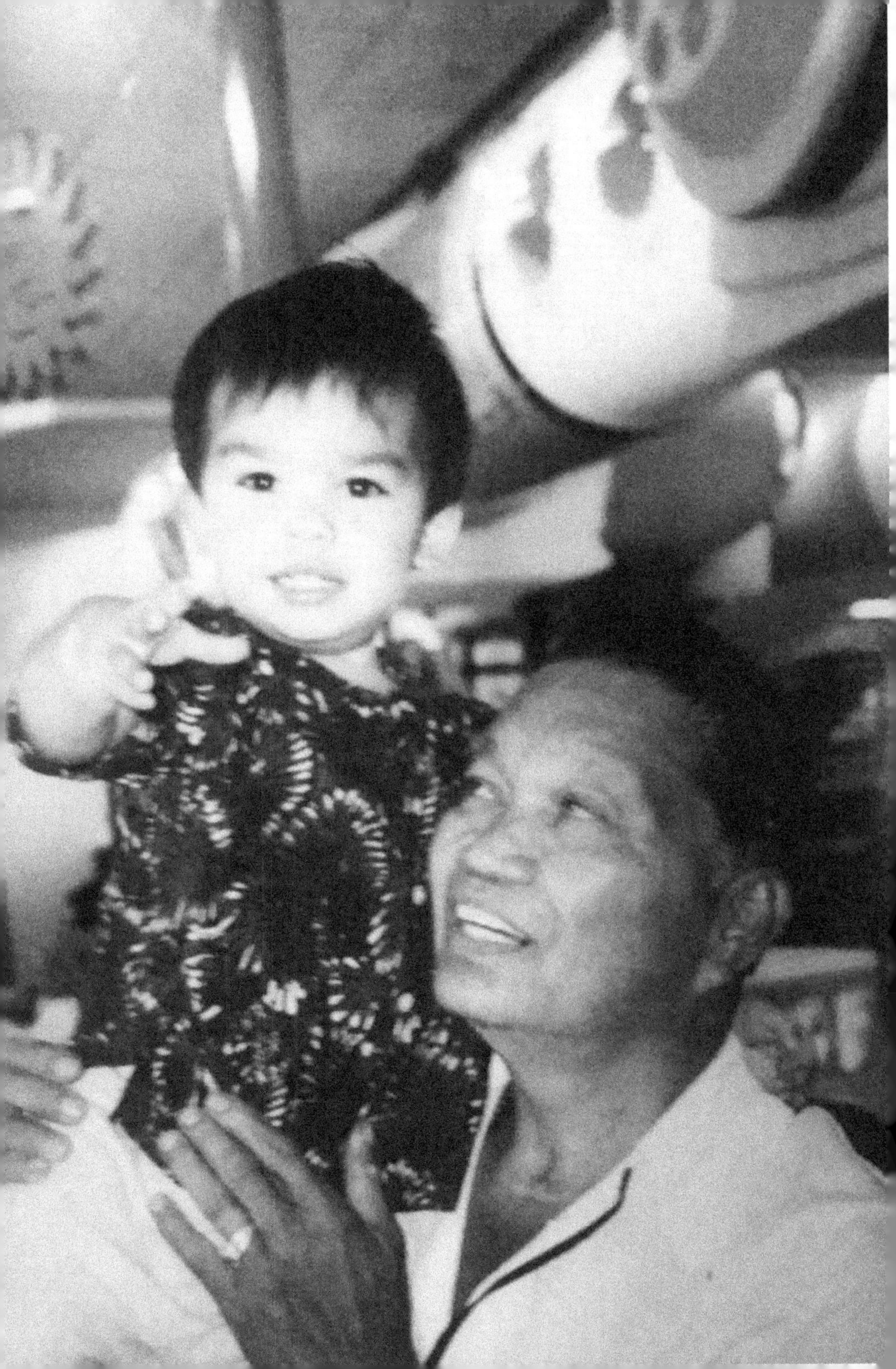

i didn't just fall in love with your flowers.

i fell in love with your roots.

i fell in love with the atmosphere that surrounded you,

i fell in love with the gravity of your presence,

i fell in love with the garden you built from scratch.

i watered he who watered others

and got nothing in return.

when i'm gone,
i hope you read back the messages you sent me,
and realize,
that you didn't care about me.
you were consumed with your selfishness.

i'm paradoxical.

i have a god complex, with no god in me.

a visionary with no vision.

a writer who hates reading.

a philosopher with no philosophy.

a jack-of-all-trades and a master of none.

i love unconditionally, with no question.

i'm dumb and poetic.

"how are you doing?"

i'm not okay. next question.

"is there anything i can do?"

no, there's nothing anyone can do. next question.

"let me know if you need anything."

thank you, but i won't.

i hate letting others see my problems.

i refuse to dim my light

to accommodate your doubts.

the goals we set

were so that, together, we could thrive.

only later did i notice,

i tore myself down so i could rebuild your broken pieces.

no more.

never again.

i never thought you would betray me.

you established otherwise.

and your reasoning?

"i don't want to regret not taking a chance on marcos."

losing someone close to you is never easy.
the air you breathe gets heavier.
waking up takes more energy than it's worth.
going about the day turns into survival.
life seems to continue,
whether you want it to or not.
it's up to you to determine what
the rest of your journey looks like.

equivalent exchange states;

to obtain something, something of equal value must be given.

so,

why didn't you love me as much as i loved you?

why didn't you fight for us like i did?

why were you selfish when i was selfless?

why were you a vile person when i was good to you?

why didn't you give me the same effort i gave you?

and why did you give him, everything you never gave me...

we laid down to sleep.

i held your body close to mine,

skin brushing ever so subtly.

fluttered kisses across your neck,

your soft and gentle giggles that followed.

beauty captured within such a simple moment.

a moment in time that belonged only to us.

pov: you're my therapist,

"why do you keep giving everything to someone who doesn't realize the value of your sacrifices?"

i don't know, i replied.

how could you place worth on one's heart?

you can't.

one's heart is inestimable.

volunteering to enlist in the military was my choice,
and i was proud of it until i met you.

because, presently,

the guilt of not being by your side,
chips away at my soul piece by piece.

i used to love the idea
of other people loving me.
i would be the people pleaser
or try to fit in to be likable.

now,

i could care less
about the opinions of others.
i only care about
the man who stares back at me
when i look in the mirror.

who in your life, could you say, loves you *unconditionally?*

don't lie.

i acknowledged that you <u>had</u> to go.
you couldn't walk on the same path as me anymore.
it's not because you weren't worthy enough
or you didn't belong beside me,

quite the opposite. that's where you were meant to be.

but as my final act of love,
i let you go.
instead of fighting
or trying to persuade you to stay,

unpretentiously, i let you go.

you leaving reminded me of
one of the foremost perspectives i once held,

this world doesn't deserve a good person like me,
because my kindness only gets trampled over.

so this time,
i choose not to be a part of it anymore.

no longer will i be a possibility

for you to run back to

when you fall.

as much as i'd rather lose every piece of myself

than to see you disappear completely,

my heart can't handle

another person who treats me

like an option you'd choose,

when you have nothing left.

one day i felt something in my head

that was unmistakable.

it was like a tighly wound string

suddenly snapped.

i smile again to distract,

laughed every day so i seemed okay,

and reverted to the *good person* people knew me as.

i love you, yesterday, today, and forever

i remember now.
it was my sanity
that broke.

hopefully my absence
will showcase my worth,
more than my presence
appeared to lack.

to my fellow brothers and sisters in arms

thank you for the service you gave to this country.
greater than that, thank you,
for the untold sacrifices you made.
especially the mental battles that no one knows about.
i'm sorry for any hardships or suffering
those sacrifices may have caused.
standing beside you today,
i am immensely proud
of your dedication to propel yourself forward
and your daily fight.

i love you, yesterday, today, and forever

my life's purpose has always been
service to others.
having someone to devote my all to
amplifies the value of my existence.

similarly,

it is for these reasons
why i could never be alone.
for what could equal the value
of another person's companionship?

now,

i have to live knowing
that i used to build dreams about you.

in those dreams,

i'd hold you closer, if only for a brief moment,
because i knew that when i woke,
you would no longer be there.

if *you* texted...

if *you* called...

if *you* showed up to my door...

if *you* needed me...

i'd reply

i'd answer

i'd let you in

i'd be there

that's just who i am

and that's who i'll always be

did you know how strong i was?

not physically,

but emotionally and mentally.

did you know the stories,

that later became the foundation

of my strength...?

if only you knew.

because then, you'd understand

why i was so exhausted with life.

one of the biggest lessons you ever taught me...

love,

will never be enough.

consistency,

the key to my heart.

reassurance,

the healing of my traumas.

loyalty,

the foundation for my love.

empathy,

the cradle to my understanding.

patience,

my love language.

i let you lose me.

holding the door open

so you could walk away.

in those days,

you didn't care about losing me.

you felt like you

were better off without me.

and maybe, just maybe,

you were.

when someone is depressed

and their mood suddenly changes,

they seem happier out of nowhere,

they appear more outspoken,

and it's almost like they're back to their usual self...

check on them,

it's a silent cry for help,

they're about to **give up**.

it's okay, after a while,

i started expecting the bare minimum from you.

i'm no longer surprised

by the things you do or say.

i'm just disappointed.

if you ever feel

like i'm "calling you out of your name."

i'm not insulting you;

i'm describing you.

there's a very distinct difference.

for as long as i can remember,

people have always come to me,

becuase they know i'll always respond.

if someone needed me,

i'd be there without hesitation.

if someone had a question,

i'd answer or find the answer.

i'm dependable,

because i know how it feels

to call on someone and have no reply.

i'll ensconce myself within the clouds;

weightless and free.

floating around without a care in the world.

the angels are beckoning,

and it's time for me to go home.

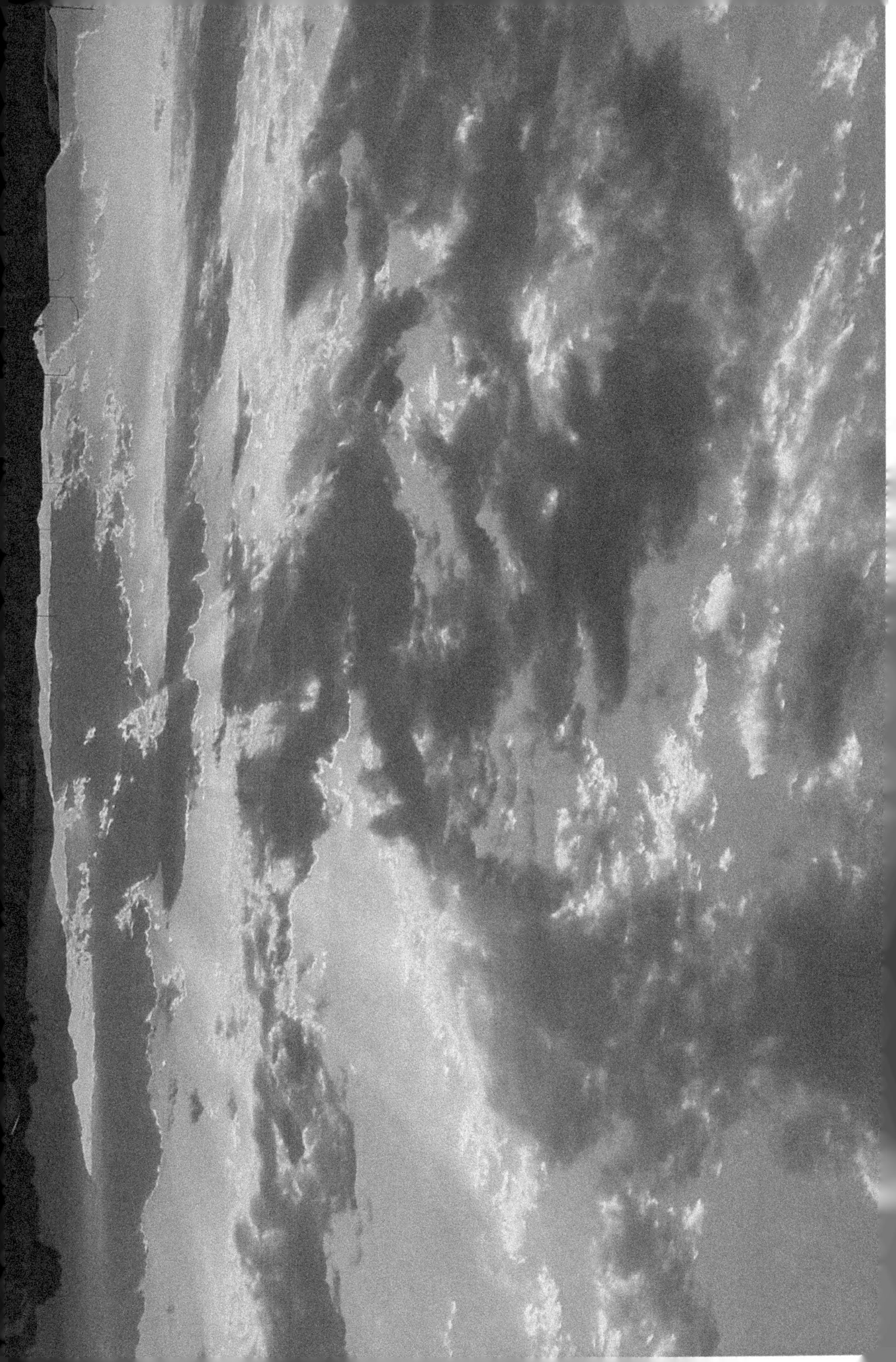

stop. being. there. for. people. who. only. take. advantage. of. you.

<u>READ THAT SHIT AGAIN</u>

oh, i see now...

you painted their red flags green,

probably to convince yourself they're good for you.

you know...

over time, that paint, will fade,

along with the false feelings you had for them.

without saying it, i begged you to stay.

i composed paragraph after paragraph

and deployed them on the battlefield

of our failed relationship.

it was, by far, the most remarkable delusion i had.

to think that mere words,

could ever make you love me again.

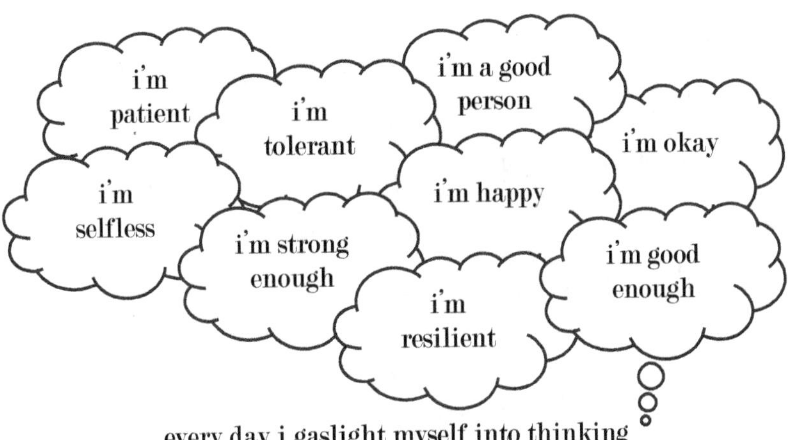

every day i gaslight myself into thinking

the thought that,

we only exist within brief moments

is simply...

transcendental.

throughout my time here,

i've stitched myself

into the fabric of people's hearts.

hoping that, one day,

the red thread of fate

would reveal my soul

to you.

the space in between.

butterflies and lilac.

april showers, dancing.

there, my love, blossoms.

ages 17 – 18,

you enlist.

ages 18 – 19,

you get married.

ages 19 – 20,

you get your first divorce.

ages 20 – 21,

you come out and get raped on your first deployment.

ages 21 – 22,

you struggle learning how to be alone, and fail.

ages 22 – 23,

you meet your forever boy.

ages 23 – 24,

you marry him, and you're happy again.

ages 24 – 25,

you start building your futures together.

ages 25 – 26,

you get your second divorce.

age 26,

you remember your true purpose.

for some, judment forms

in the actions of your weakest moment.

for me, judgment forms

in the consistency of those actions.

my beautiful Emma-Rose.

holding you for the first time emptied the breath from my lungs.

how something as fragile as life itself

could embody the essence of everything so pure in this world.

beauty becomes you with every passing day,

from your dark brown eyes

to your rosy red cheeks.

"i love you uncle jojo" sets my heart ablaze,

and flushes my face with tears.

as you get older, i can only hope,

you'll never forget that

uncle jojo loves you so much more.

seeing the effort you've put forth there

in only two months,

ignited a deep-rooted rage within my heart.

especially because

in the three years of our relationship,

you barely put in that effort.

you got comfortable and then blamed me for it.

a long time ago,

i learned to rest when i got tired

instead of giving up.

how long do you think

i had to rest

before i actually called it quits?

i'm a prideful son-of-a-bitch.

i spent a long time working to change that,

because pride births arrogance.

nevertheless,

i want all the attention,

i want to be noticed by everyone,

i want to be fawned over,

i want to be cried over,

i want to be cared for,

i wanted to be loved.

and then i remembered i was never alone

scan me

when i'm gone from this world,

i know i'll live on.

pieces and parts of me

will exist in the hearts and minds of so many.

memories and moments

shared with friends, family, and strangers.

so let me ask you,

which version of me lives rent-free in your head?

stop expecting others to reciprocate the same love you give.

stop expecting others to reciprocate the same love you give.

stop expecting others to reciprocate the same love you give.

stop expecting others to reciprocate the same love you give.

stop expecting others to reciprocate the same love you give.

stop expecting others to reciprocate the same love you give.

stop expecting others to reciprocate the same love you give.

stop expecting others to reciprocate the same love you give.

stop expecting others to reciprocate the same love you give.

stop expecting others to reciprocate the same love you give.

stop expecting others to reciprocate the same love you give.

stop expecting others to reciprocate the same love you give.

stop expecting others to reciprocate the same love you give.

stop expecting others to reciprocate the same love you give.

stop expecting others to reciprocate the same love you give.

stop expecting others to reciprocate the same love you give.

stop expecting others to reciprocate the same love you give.

stop expecting others to reciprocate the same love you give.

got it yet?

it was such a simple moment...

laying in his bed,

wrapped within the warmth of his skin.

like a scene from a movie,

our faces drew close, guided by desire.

my fingers brushing his cheek,

his, tracing the contours of my back.

the soft touch of his lips on mine

left me breathless.

i could not help but smile,

as i got lost in his green eyes.

that moment was a dream,

i never wanted to wake from.

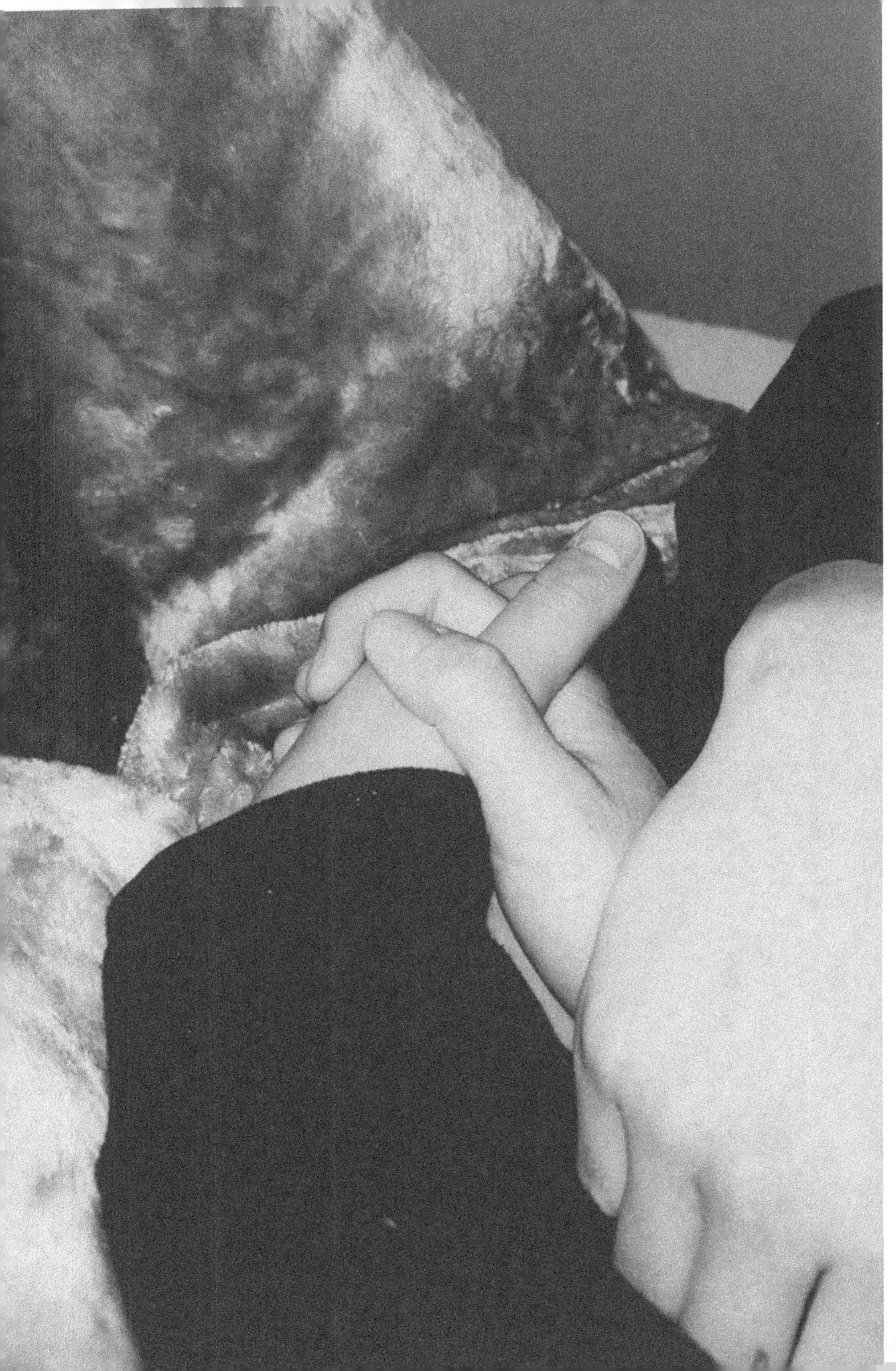

the shadow of you traces my life,

emptiness in everything we once shared.

coming home to a deafening silence,

sleeping next to a ghost,

smiling at myself in the mirror,

persuading and deceiving my mind,

laughing in the corner until i cry.

the ever-looming presence of what once was,

towers over me with immeasurable height.

the sad thing is,

i know there's a part of you

that's still in love with me.

a part of your heart you've locked away —

so you don't have to be reminded,

of how "comfortable" i am.

so you don't remember,

the tepidness of my love.

so you don't recollect,

all the happy moments we created.

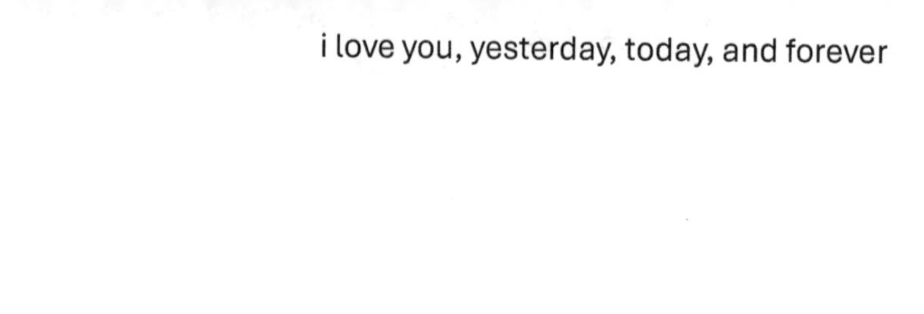

if you've ever told yourself, "right person, wrong time,"

i just wanted to let you know that...

if they were truly the right person,

then there would never be a wrong time.

i wish my eyes could take pictures.

so i could show you,

the beauty that captivated me every day.

and

the hell you caused when you walked away.

how do i explain that the voices never stop?

that even when i'm happy, i still hear the whispers.

it's like tinnitus gifted to me by the devil.

ringing these thoughts in my ears —

maybe i was okay in another life,

maybe i didn't have to suffer so much,

maybe you and i stayed together,

maybe i didn't attempt suicide seven times,

maybe i was enough,

maybe i didn't give up,

maybe. just maybe.

and there i was.

balled up on the shower floor –

water cascading, soothing my sin.

washing away the evil thoughts i let in.

"what was i to you?"

selling a gold wedding ring –

pawning off my memory for a quick buck.

so that you know...

it was easier to convince myself

that you didn't care about me at all,

rather than believe

that you still cared and chose to hurt me

over and over again.

there is a fundamental distinctiveness between

those who talk to you on their free time

and

those who free their time to talk to you.

and then there are

those assholes who talk to you when it's convenient.

fuck those guys.

time heals all wounds, yes, but on the other hand,

time reveals motive.

time exposes truth.

time ties the noose around your neck.

time pushes the chair from beneath you.

time and time again,

cleans your clock and finishes what it started.

you closed my book before i finished writing.

and so the time has come

for me to release the grip on my pen.

i guess our story ends here,

a pieced-together and messy ending.

at least our paths crossed,

and i was able to author a few chapters.

you,

you were one of my favorite characters.

too many people have become painful reminders

that i love too deeply,

care too much,

and sacrifice

far more

than i ever should.

i tried to rise from the ashes of that

charred garden.

you filled my lungs with loneliness

and suffocated me with your smile.

i feel numb –

the emptiness engulfed my heart.

it'll take 6 people to carry my casket

down the aisle for all to see.

        it'll take 4 people to spread my ashes

          at my final resting place.

                but it only took 1 person,

                  to put me there.

you **are** **not** the product of what happened to you; you alone choose what you
are.

happiness within words, unexpressed.

the mirror reflects intent.

unenvisiaged hope unravels like a ball of twine.

isn't it funny how people only begin to hear you

when you're dead?

you replay those final conversations

and wonder if you could've changed the outcome.

their memory seems to weigh on you,

shackling you to the reality that you'll *never*

hear from them again.

"Late, Late."

- Terry Rodas

be careful who you trust,

you could be off fighting a war

and the person you love the most,

leaves you.

- sincerely, a broken heart

in-yun

[korean]

with every passing lifetime, we shall meet again.

be it ten or ten thousand.

the fate of our souls will brush each other –

a red string tethers you to me.

this, too, shall pass.

will you leave fortunes from cookies

within the pages of my books?

i sat there in my truck,

head tilted back, eyes closed.

breathing getting heavier and heavier,

fighting the urge to text him.

text him to see if he replies – or not.

not wanting to walk up the stairs

to a desolate apartment once littered

with our laughter.

now only haunted by your ghost.

your insecurities don't magically disappear

just because you're in a relationship.

even if you work on them

or your partner makes you feel secure.

insecurities are part of what makes us human —

remember that before you blame someone

for "not changing."

if you told me i'd die tomorrow,

i'd laugh.

no goodbyes,

no final words,

no hesitation.

i'd vanish like a shadow in the night.

as much as i've written about

sadness, death, and depression.

i still can't convey the loss of you

that i experience every day.

it's indescribable.

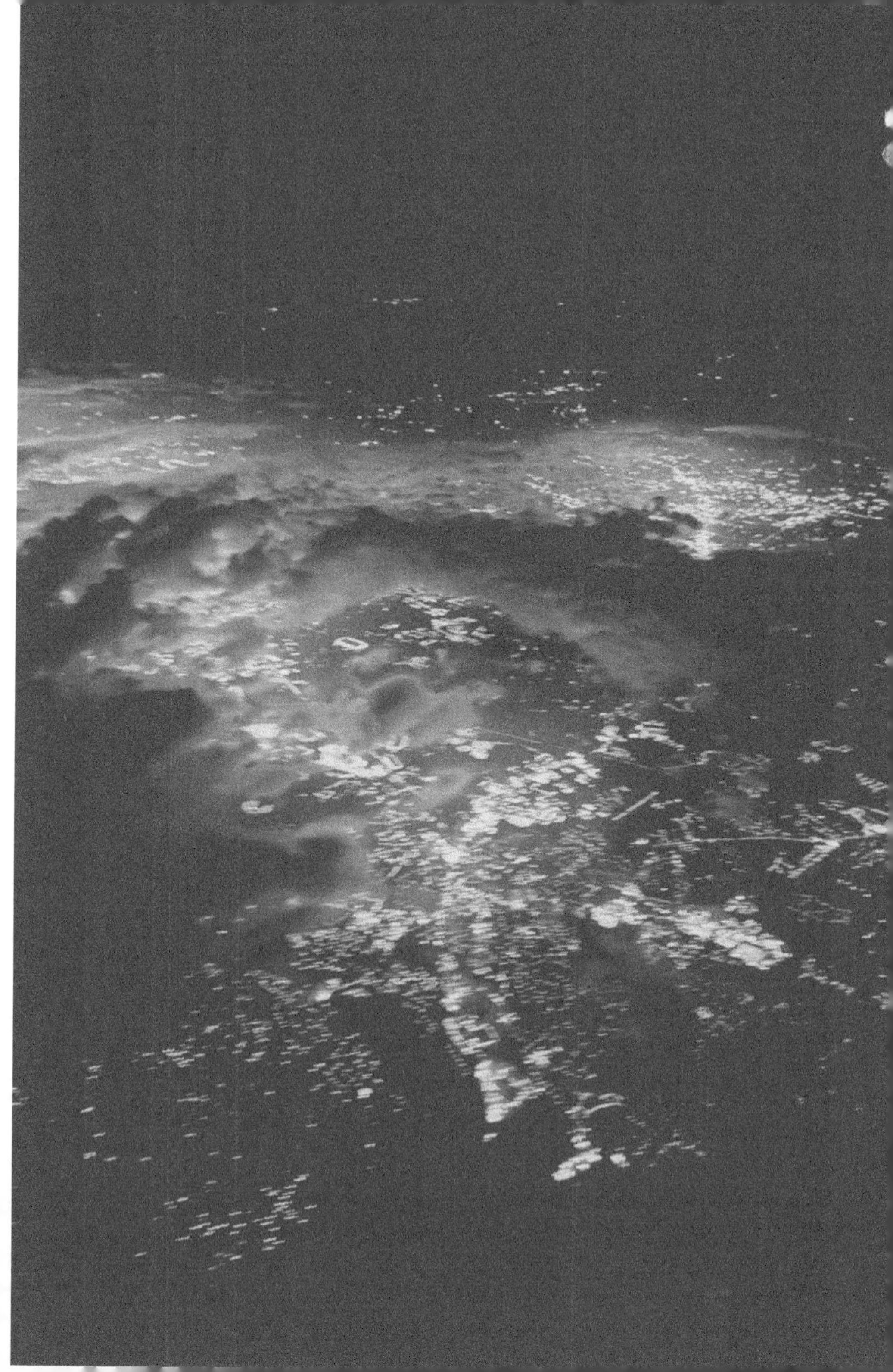

it was cloudy today.

thunder always comes before lightning.

the pitter-patter of rain – dead man walking.

all i remembered was sprinting.

i ran and ran and ran and ran...

you were my finish line, or at least i wanted you to be.

god, i really wanted you to be.

nothing bad anyone says about me ever mattered,

because i guarantee i've looked in the mirror

and said much worse.

he whispered,

"sweet dreams, beautiful boy."

as he pulled my body closer to his.
it had felt like an eternity
since someone made me feel safe.

the moon was lost in your sky,

because you were too busy

entertaining a star,

thinking they were the one.

a lot of things happen in our lives that make no sense,

but there's a melancholic allure to its mystery.

even if i'm no longer your person,

you will always be my person.

i will be there for you no matter what.

that's one promise i'll never break.

what we had wasn't imaginary,

it was real.

it was chemistry.

it was vibrant.

it was everything to me.

very often, i think i'm only meant to give love

and not receive it.

i deserve to be loved the same way i love others,

i don't think i will.

one of the hardest things i've done

was letting go of someone

knowing full and well they won't come back.

there's grace in our tragedy —

our lore expressed the dichotomies of life.

loneliness and togetherness.

happiness and sadness.

security and insecurity.

loyalty and disloyalty.

love and hate.

the key to your growth does not lie in not making mistakes.

it lies in your apperception –

to know which mistakes are worth the accompanying lessons.

a few years passed between us before we met again. it was cold, that day in december.

"are you in love?" he asked.

"i was." i replied.

i yearn for our halcyon moments.

like a blank canvas adorned with gentle pastels.

moments where you stole my attention,

moments where your soul was ethereal,

moments where you were my favorite distraction,

moments where your giggles were winsome.

those are the moments

my heart longs for.

you. are an enigma.

i heard your voice again and suddenly...

my heart melted like wax beside a flame.

all that pain seemed to disappear,

if only for an instant.

wisdom

is

only

granted

to

those

who

experience

life

in

it's

purest

form.

7,100 known spoken languages exist today, yet none contain words that accurately depict the chaos in my head. arcane in nature – desperate are my attempts to convey the unexplainable.

i'm trapped.

i'm screaming.

can anyone hear me?

help...

the voices won't stop.

what has life turned into.

i'm constantly at war

with who i see in the mirror.

regardless of the victor,

i still lose.

turn your eyes away from me

for all you will feast,

is the afterimage of a man.

the crown of thorns making its home upon his head,

chains binding his wrists,

and blood that runs from his eyes.

maturing is realizing that,

while i made some mistakes, i was accountable.

i was never the issue –

you, however, only blamed me for the past

you forgave me for.

your hands were so warm,

but your heart was so cold.

homesick for something

that only exists in my dreams.

i realized

the apology i needed from you

is one i'll never get.

and i think that made it sting

that much more.

woe are the trees

which gives us oxygen,

only to be executed

by the greed of all humankind.

i've approached a point where

i'm not happy nor am i sad.

i'm just empty. blank.

157

your existence shattered the laws of my reality.

admitting i was awestruck would be an understatement.

oh. i forgot to tell you...

remember who the fuck you are!

you are the sun, the moon, the stars,

and all the space that encompasses them.

your existence shattered the laws to my reality.

admitting i was awestruck is an understatement.

~~i'm~~ you're strong because ~~i~~ you want to be.

~~i'm~~ you're strong becuase ~~i've~~ you've been weak.

~~i'm~~ you're not patient by choice,

~~i'm~~ you're patient because ~~i've~~ you've rushed things.

~~i'm~~ you're not a good person for the title,

~~i'm~~ you're a good person because ~~i've~~ you've been treated like shit.

~~i'm~~ you're not scared anymore,

because ~~i've~~ you've let fear control ~~me~~ you for way too long.

when i love...

    i love hard.

        like really fucking hard.

            i give so much that love consumes me

                within every facet of its concept.

it was cold that evening. the clouds, amber in color as the sun illuminates their silhouette.

"do you want to kill yourself?"

i stood there in utter disbelief and recall wondering if he could read my mind.

"of course not."

"i'm going to be selfish and ask you. please don't..."

the silence that followed reverberated throughout each atom in my body. my heart, pounding against my ribcage like japanese taiko drums preparing for war.

"i think i'm going to be selfish too,"

i thought to myself.

the thoughts,
as i talked to myself

"Why is love intensified by absence?"

Love is one of those emotions that can either be fickle or powerful. Everyone falls in love at some point in their lives, and as unique as these experiences are, the emotion is the same across the board. Love can be a double-edged sword for someone like me, whose life purpose is caring for someone else.

When I say "double-edged," I mean that when I love someone, I love immeasurably and unconditionally, which can hurt all the more when that person leaves. Although I was very young, I loved my father's parents, Apo Pennie and Apo Solon, a great deal. Moreso, when my Apo Solon died, it felt as though a small dark void had developed within my soul that never went away. I had gone waking up next to him a couple of years ago, cooking beside him, watering the garden, and doing almost everything with him.

I think absence intensifies love, which proves it is indeed love. It is often said, "If you truly love someone, you can let them go." As much animosity as I have for this saying, I also agree with it only in the sense of death. The feeling of their absence will be comparable to how intensely you loved them.

This bastard named, Trevis, once asked me,

"How do you receive people after what you've been through?"

Openly and without reservation. It never mattered to me how much betrayal or pain I've suffered. When you receive someone new while clutching your past in your fists, you're more likely to punch them at the first sign of misgiving. You'll hold preconceived notions against them before you learn who they are. That's similar to judging a book by its cover simply because you've read another book that resembles it.

We've all been hurt by someone, but that doesn't mean the next person will hurt you. While we share similarities, we're unique in our own right and deserve a fresh slate. If someone treated you in that way, you might be able to understand it, but the impalpable distrust that is sewn in that first encounter would be just as loud as an explosion.

Let it be he who casts the first stone; otherwise, allow yourself the ability to receive someone unburdened. Only then can you recognize the hidden beauty within each person's soul. In my opinion, it's crucial to approach others with not only an open mind, but a willngness to view them from different perspectives. You're not a mind reader, are you? So how could you judge them before you've listened to the story that molded them into who they are?

"Is the hardest part of losing someone the goodbye or learning to live without them?"

The answer is dependent on a few things. Was the "goodbye" mutual? How deeply did you love this person? How much of your lives were engrained in each other's? Remember, everyone will have their answer to this question, generally based on their recollections.

From experience, I'd say learning to live without them has been more difficult. That's only because I don't leave anyone; the other person always leaves me. I'm left to pick up the pieces in a place once built by two people, so I have to experience the "goodbye" and the emptiness thereafter. I think it's because I love being unfettered and giving my all in every relationship I'm in that when someone leaves, I have to restart.

I find myself rebuilding a life that significant others are constantly tearing down. Within this reconstruction, I'm plagued with thoughts of disdain and depression even though I know that I was always more than good enough. Learning to live without them has always been more painful because that's when I realized just how much I loved that person.

The "goodbye" can be painful or feel like a breath of fresh air that opens you up to new possibilities.

"If the world were ending, who would you call first to say "I love you"?"

I wouldn't call anyone. As much as I love many people in my life, I wouldn't reach out in those final moments. I'd sit there and embrace the icy touch of Death alone. If I still had someone to care for, I'd turn to him and say it.

On the other hand, I would keep my phone close to me just in case it turns out to be someone's last call. While I know most people would call someone else, I could be surprised by who would call me.

It's within that uncertainty that I find genuine happiness.

"What? Are you afraid of making the connections you were born to make?"

It isn't that I am afraid of making those connections. As a matter of fact, it was in all of those connections that I discovered what divine happiness was. Being present for others – showing up – listening to their stories – in the words of my bright younger brother, "the purest form of life is a mosaic of moments."

I'm simply tired of making all of these connections and not getting the love that I know I deserve. I'm tired of giving it my all only to realize later that what I give, I likely will not receive. At the ripe young age of 26, I experienced two of the supposed three great loves of my life. The first was while I was a young teenager budding into adulthood. The second, while I was more than prepared to settle down and build the rest of my future. Both loves were phenomenal in their respects, but the one thing that remained consistent was they left me for someone else in the end.

I'll not pretend to be a perfect person. I made my mistakes, but I loved far greater and remained accountable. I wondered how much more I could've given so often that it drove me into bouts of anxiety and imposter syndrome. So when I confide in others and I'm met with the response, "But you're still not done yet," "You have more happiness to spread," "There are more fish in the sea," "You'll find the right one, one day." It absolutely crushes my soul.

I'm simply tired... And I'm done.

Author's note

I published these books so that a physical piece of me remained in this world after I departed. It is undoubtedly the most selfish act I have ever committed to and arguably my proudest.

We live in a paradoxical world, and our lives are governed by emotion. Depression has challenged me all my life, and I found a way to articulate how I feel and then write it down for all to bear witness. I hope that when someone reads one of my poems, they can feel the words seep into the essence of their soul and find a place within their hearts.

I'll offer no apology for what happens next because I know I will be happy and free for the first time in a long while. Free to roam the unknown. Free to unravel the hereafter.

I dedicate this to those of you who saw me past the mask I wore and the façade I presented.